Is It Time Yet?

A Family Advent Journey

Written by Bethany Darwin
Illustrated by Jedidjah Rotter

For Obadiah
I pray you will fall more and more
in love with Jesus each year!

Thank You
I want to thank my husband, Joseph, for the
way he encouraged me in this project.

I want to thank my parents who always made
Christmas about Jesus. And, I want to thank
my mom for sharing her love of collecting
nativity scenes with me.

Is It Time Yet?: A Family Advent Journey
Bethany Darwin
2020
Self-published
(bethany@sundayschoolstore.com)

Scripture references are taken from the ESV version of the Bible

All rights reserved.
No part of this publication may be reproduced, stored in a retrieval system, stored in a database and / or published in any form or by any means, electronic, mechanical, photocopying, recording or otherwise, without the prior written permission of the publisher.

Dear Parents,

Thank you for deciding to make "Is It Time Yet?" a part of your family's Christmas celebration. Children are naturally anticipatory and always seem to be looking forward to the next big event. So, why not capitalize on that refrain of *is it time yet* and use it to point children to Christ.

In this book, you'll find 25 stories meant to be read 1 per day, December 1-25. Each story stands alone, but together they tell the overarching story of the Bible, help children to see that Jesus came at just the right time, and remind us each day that Christmas is more about Jesus on the cross than Jesus in the manger.

A simple reading of the story will only take a few minutes a day, or you can use the reading as part of a family worship time using the accompanying "Is It Time Yet? Family Worship Guide." This guide is available free of charge using the code **WORSHIP25** at **sundayschool.store**. Also available on the store is an accompanying coloring and activity book and a 4-week curriculum perfect for Sunday School or homeschool during the advent season.

Bethany

Table of Contents

 December 1 — Galatians 4:4-5 & Luke 2

 December 2 — John 1

 December 3 — Genesis 1 & 2

 December 4 — Genesis 3

 December 5 — Genesis 6-9

 December 6 — Genesis 11

 December 7 — Genesis 12, 15, 18 & 21

 December 8 — Genesis 22

 December 9 — Genesis 37 - 50

 December 10 — Exodus 1

 December 11 — Exodus 3

 December 12 — Exodus 12

	December 13	Exodus 20
	December 14	Numbers 13 & 14
	December 15	Joshua 2
	December 16	Ruth
	December 17	1 Samuel 16
	December 18	1 Samuel 17
	December 19	1 Kings 18
	December 20	Jonah
	December 21	Isaiah 7, 9, 53
	December 22	reflect on past readings
	December 23	Luke 1
	December 24	Luke 2
	December 25	Luke 23

What time is it?
Seriously, go check. I'll wait.

Time is how you know when things happen. For example, you know that if you wake up at 2 in the morning it's not time for breakfast. There is a right time for everything.

Breakfast is at 7, school is at 8 and my favorite time of all is 2:30.... snack time!

Everything has a perfect

In the Bible, in Galatians 4:4-5 we read:
But when the fullness of time had come, God sent forth his Son, born of woman, born under the law, to redeem those who were under the law, so that we might receive adoption as sons.

More simply put, we could say... When the right time had come,
God sent Jesus into the world. He was born as a baby to live as a man. Jesus came to rescue God's people from sin, death, and the penalty of breaking God's law. Jesus came to bring them home as God's children.

You may know the story of Jesus coming into the world, but before we start singing 'Happy Birthday,' we need to know the rest of the story to understand why it was the right time.

Galatians 4:4-5 and Luke 2

IN THE BEGINNING.

Those are the first three words of the greatest story ever.
But, even more important is the next word.

GOD

It's the most important word in the story, because this is His story.

The Bible is the story of God.
The Bible is the story of God rescuing His people.

The story starts by telling us that God is there.

Before anything there is God.

God is eternal. He has always been and he will always be.

And this is **HIS STORY.**

So, is it time yet?

No, the story has just begun, but what a beginning it is!

John 1

And then God spoke into the darkness.
God spoke into the emptiness. God spoke into the silence.

God spoke and made the world. God spoke simple words, 'let there be light.' And there was light. God spoke and

GOD MADE.

God spoke and made light. God spoke and made land and seas. God spoke and made day and night and the sun, moon and stars. God spoke and made plants. God spoke and made birds, fish, and all the animals from the smallest mouse to the tallest giraffe. And then, God made people.

God made **THE WORLD.**

And, God made it all good. Nothing was bad. Nothing was sad.

So, is it time yet?
No, at that time, God's good people lived in God's perfect place and had a perfect relationship with Him.

Genesis 1 & 2

One day, God's enemy, the serpent, came to the man and woman in the garden and told them to eat. He told them to eat from the tree in the middle of the garden. He told them that if they ate from the tree they would become like God.

The woman ate and she gave some to the man. That was the first **SIN**.

God's people had broken God's one rule and their relationship would never be the same again.
God punished the serpent.
God punished the man.
God punished the woman.

AND, God promised that one day, a man would crush the serpent and make everything good again.

So, is it time yet?
Not yet. The man and the woman, Adam and Eve, were sent away from God's perfect place and away from God's presence. But, they left with a promise that one day, when the time was right, a Rescuer would come.

In the garden, everything was perfect. Outside the garden, everything went from bad to worse. Sin kept ruling.

Genesis 6-9

Many years passed and it seemed like things couldn't get any worse.

God chose one man, a man named Noah, to start over with him. Noah obeyed God and built an ark (a really BIG boat). Then God brought some of all the animals to the ark and closed the door. In the ark were pairs of animals and Noah and his family.

God made it rain for **40 DAYS** and nights.

Everyone and everything not in the ark died. Only those inside the ark were saved. When the rain stopped, God opened the door and Noah and his family worshipped God.

Then God made a **PROMISE.**

God put a rainbow in the sky and promised that He would never again destroy the whole world with a flood.

So, is it time yet?
No. God wiped away the sin in Noah's day, but the flood only covered sin up, it didn't get rid of it. God promised to never flood the WHOLE world again. That promise also had hope that one day God would get rid of sin forever!

After the flood, the world was new again. God had wiped away everything except Noah, his family, and some of every kind of animal. But, even though Noah and his family loved and worshipped God, sin was still there.

God told them to spread out and fill the earth. Their job was to represent God to the world.

But, before long people decided to **DISOBEY GOD.**

They decided to stay together.
They decided to build a big city.
They decided to build a tall tower.
They wanted everyone to see them.

As they were building their tall tower, God stopped them. God wanted them to obey Him. God wanted them to look to Him instead of people looking at them.

God made it so they couldn't understand each other when they talked.
God made them all speak different **LANGUAGES.**

Since they couldn't understand each other, they stopped building the tower and did what God told them to do in the first place. They spread out and filled the earth.

> So, is it time yet?
> No, not yet. First, the world was filled with people, some who obeyed God and many who did not.

Genesis 11

After God stopped the building of the tower, there were people spread out all over the world. They spoke different languages. They were becoming different nations of people.

One day, God spoke to a man named Abraham and told Abraham to follow Him. God promised to make Abraham into a great nation.

Genesis 12, 15, 18 & 21

Abraham **OBEYED.**

He took his wife and they followed where God led.

Abraham and his wife Sarah were both very old and didn't have any children. They didn't know how, but they believed that somehow God would make them into a great nation.

One day, God told Abraham to go outside and look at the stars.
God told Abraham to count them if he could.

God **PROMISED** that Abraham would have as many descendants as the stars in the sky. God also promised to give a good land and a home to Abraham's descendants.

But most importantly, God promised Abraham that one of his descendants would be the one who would bless all the nations. He would be the one they were waiting for.

When Abraham and Sarah were 100 and 90 years old, God gave them a baby named Isaac.

> So, is it time yet?
> Not yet. Isaac was the start of God fulfilling His promise to Abraham, but the real fulfillment of God's promise was still to come through another baby who would be born into Abraham's family.

Isaac was the promised son. He was the one Abraham was waiting for. It would be through Isaac that God would keep his promise to make Abraham into a great nation.

Abraham loved Isaac so much. But God wanted Abraham to **LOVE HIM** more than Isaac.

One day, God asked Abraham to take Isaac, his only son, the one he loved, and sacrifice him. God wanted Abraham to kill Isaac to show that he loved God more than Isaac.

Abraham took wood and fire and a knife, and he and Isaac went to the place where they would worship God and sacrifice.

As they got closer, Isaac asked where the lamb for the sacrifice was. Abraham simply said that God would **PROVIDE.**

Abraham placed his son, the one he loved, on the wood on the altar. But, before he could kill him, God stopped him. In the bushes was a ram. God said to sacrifice it instead of Isaac.

Abraham had shown God he loved Him more than his son. Abraham loved God more than the promises God had made.

So, is it time yet? No. But, the way that Isaac was rescued, pointed to the way that God would rescue His people through the Rescuer who was coming. The Lamb died in the place of God's people.

Genesis 22

God provided a ram to die in the place of Isaac. God began to fulfill His promise to Abraham through Isaac that He would give him a large family, one of whom would save the world.

Isaac grew up, got married, and had two sons, Jacob and Esau.
Jacob grew up, got married, and had twelve sons, Reuben, Simeon, Levi, Judah, Issachar, Zebulun, Dan, Naphtali, Gad, Asher, Joseph, and Benjamin.

Joseph and Benjamin were Jacob's favorite sons.
Jacob gave Joseph a special brightly colored coat.
God gave Joseph dreams about his brothers bowing down to him.

The dreams and the special coat from his dad made the other brothers very jealous. One day, they sold Joseph to slave traders and tore up Joseph's coat to make it look like animals had attacked Joseph.

Joseph was taken to Egypt. Joseph's brothers thought they had won, but this was all part of God's **RESCUE PLAN.**

In Egypt, Joseph was a servant, then a prisoner and then he became second in command to the Pharaoh. God used Joseph in Egypt to provide food to rescue his family from starvation.

> So, is it time yet?
> Nope. It still wasn't time. Joseph was a descendant of Abraham who rescued God's people, but an even greater rescue was still to come!

Genesis 37-50

Years passed after God used Joseph to rescue His special family. They came down to Egypt as a family of 70. But generations came and went and they were still in Egypt.

God prospered them and before long there were so many of them that the Pharaoh started to worry. The Pharaoh didn't want them to be in charge, so he made them into **SLAVES.**

Exodus 1

For 400 years, God's special family were slaves in Egypt. They were made to work hard for the Egyptians, but God prospered them. Even when the Pharaoh made their work almost impossible, God kept prospering them.

No matter what, they never forgot God's promise. God had made them into a great nation, just like he had promised Abraham. But what about the rest of the promise?

How was God going to give them land when they were in Egypt?
And how would God give them a home when they were slaves?

God had a plan and it all started with the birth of a **BABY**.

So, is it time yet?
It sounds like it. A special descendant of Abraham was coming to rescue God's people. But, this baby wasn't the Promised Rescuer they were waiting for. This rescue plan started with the birth of a baby named Moses.

When Moses grew up, he didn't know where he fit; with the Hebrews or with the Egyptians? So, after killing an Egyptian to protect a Hebrew, he ran away to Midian where he worked as a shepherd for years.

One day while out with the sheep, he saw a bush that was on fire but not being burned up. As he approached the bush to see what was happening, a voice spoke to him from the bush.

It was God!
The God of Abraham.
The God of Isaac.
The God of Jacob.
God introduced Himself to Moses. God called Himself

He said, "I Am your God. I am rescuing you."

God had heard His people crying out to be saved in Egypt.
God was coming to their rescue.
God was sending Moses to lead them out of slavery.

So, is it time yet?
No. God spoke to His people and God sent Moses to rescue them.
But when the time was right, God Himself came to rescue His people and lead them home to Himself.

God used Moses to show His power to the Egyptians through a series of plagues. Through frogs and gnats and locusts and hail and blood in the river and horrible sores and darkness, God showed that He alone has power over all of creation.

Most importantly, God showed that He is more powerful than all the fake gods the Egyptians worshipped. But still, the Pharaoh refused to listen. The Pharaoh refused to let God's people leave.

Through Moses, God told His people to do something radical. He told them that each household should kill a **LAMB** and paint the lamb's blood around the doorposts of their house.

Then God told them to go in and wait.

That night, God passed through the land. God passed right over all the homes with lamb's blood on the door. But, in the homes without the blood of a lamb, the firstborn son died. Throughout the land of Egypt, family after family grieved the death of a beloved son, while God's people rejoiced that the lamb **DIED** in their place.

The next day, the Pharaoh sent God's people out of his land.
God had rescued them and He was taking them home.

> So, is it time yet?
> Not quite. The blood of the lambs saved God's people on that dark night, but when the time was right, God sent His own beloved son and He died as the Passover lamb and saved His people forever.

Exodus 12

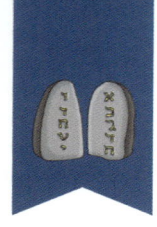

God led His people out of Egypt in a miraculous way, by opening up the sea for them to walk through on dry land. 430 years earlier, 70 members of Jacob's family had entered Egypt. On this day, hundreds of thousands left.

These people had been surrounded by Egyptian culture and laws and fake gods for generations. One of the first things God did was to make a covenant with them. God promised to be their God and that they would be His people.

But what does it mean to be God's people?
How would they know what to do?

They didn't know. So God gave them the **LAW.**

God's law showed the people how to love God.
God's law showed the people how to love each other.
God's law showed them how to be set apart from the people around them.

God wrote His law on two stone tablets and gave them to Moses on top of Mt. Sinai. These 10 commandments from God were meant to help God's people follow and obey Him.

> So, is it time yet?
> It seems like it as God and His people were together under His law. But, the people couldn't keep the law. No one can keep the law perfectly except God. But one day, God Himself came and perfectly obeyed God's law.

Exodus 20

Numbers 13-14

God taught them how to be His people as they traveled through the desert. As they neared the promised land, God told them it was time. It was time to go in and conquer the land. It was time for the promise.

Moses sent Joshua, Caleb, and 10 other men in to spy out the land. The land was full of strong men. But it was also full of good food. God was giving them a beautiful land.

But, 10 of the men (everyone except Joshua and Caleb), told the people about the big strong men. They made the people afraid.

The people were scared and didn't trust God.
The people said, "No, we can't go into the land."

So, God punished the people for not trusting Him. God said none of them would ever go into the promised land, except Joshua and Caleb. God said the rest of them would die in the desert.

For the next **40 YEARS,** the people wandered in the desert. During this time, God cared for them, but God did not give them His promise.

So, is it time yet?
Just like the promise of land went to the next generation, the promise of a forever rescue went to a generation yet to be born. Not long after this, God led them into the promise land. But, it was many years later before He gave them His Rescuer.

God led His people and cared for them for 40 years in the desert.
God used this time to teach them to be His people.

As they prepared to enter the land, God gave them a new leader - Joshua.
The land was in front of them, but how would God give it to them?
Joshua sent two men into the city of Jericho as spies.

They went in and stayed in the home of a woman named **RAHAB.**

The king heard about the spies and sent soldiers to find them.
So Rahab hid them on the roof under some stalks of flax.

When the soldiers came, Rahab said, "Yes, they were here, but they left. Go. Chase them."
And they did. They ran out of the city chasing the spies.

Rahab told the spies that she had heard about how God was leading and guiding and fighting for His people. Rahab said she believed He was the true God. Rahab asked them to save her when they came to take the city. Then, Rahab let the spies down the city wall with a **ROPE.**

About two weeks later, God led His people into Jericho with a shout and a trumpet blast. Everyone in Jericho was killed except for Rahab and her family. She became part of God's people as they moved into the promised land. God's promise started to extend outside of Abraham's family.

> So, is it time yet?
> Not yet. God's people were in God's promised land, and the promise had started extending to the world, but the people still needed to learn to look to God for rescue, the way Rahab did.

The famine was bad in the promised land, so Elimelek and Naomi and their two sons left Bethlehem and moved to Moab. While in Moab, both of their sons married Moabite women. After some time, both of the sons and Elimelek died in Moab.

Ruth

Naomi decided to return to Bethlehem and **RUTH**, one of her daughters-in-law, decided to come with her.
Ruth chose to follow Naomi's God, the true God, and join His people.

Back in Bethlehem, it was hard for the 2 women alone. Ruth went to the fields in the area and picked up bits of grain that the harvesters left behind.

One day, she was doing this in Boaz's field. He saw her and felt sorry for her, so he told his men to leave extra for her. Boaz even told his men to watch out for her and protect her.

Boaz was a relative of Elimelek.
This meant he could marry Ruth and continue Elimelek's family line.
Boaz was called a kinsman-redeemer because he was a family member who could **REDEEM** or rescue his relatives.

Boaz married Ruth and they had a son named Obed. Obed had a son named Jesse. Jesse had eight sons, the youngest was a boy named David, but that's a story for another day.

> So, is it time yet?
> In Ruth's story, we saw a glimpse of the Redeemer to come. Boaz stepped in as the redeemer of Naomi's family line by marrying Ruth. He rescued them, and one day the Promised Redeemer was born into their family line.

The people of God were getting tired of being different than the other nations. They wanted a king to rule over them. But they forgot 1 important thing. God was their God was ruling over them.

KING.

They demanded a king and God gave them a king named Saul. Saul didn't follow God with his whole heart. Saul didn't lead the people to follow God.

1 Samuel 16

So, God sent Samuel to the town of Bethlehem to the house of a man named Jesse. Does that name sound familiar? It should, Jesse was the grandson of Boaz and Ruth. Jesse had 8 sons and one of them was going to be chosen as king.

Samuel looked at 7 of the sons from oldest to youngest. Some looked like kings, but God told Samuel not to look at their outward appearance. Finally, Jesse called his youngest son, David, and Samuel said that he was the one God had chosen as king.

David ruled over God's people for 40 years. And, God promised that David's son would

REIGN FOREVER.

So, is it time yet?
Not quite. The promise of a Forever King sounded like what they were waiting for. But, Solomon wasn't the Forever King. Instead, years later, another baby was born in Bethlehem in the line of David and He rules as God's Forever King.

While David was still a young man in the service of King Saul, the Philistines attacked Israel. Saul and the army of Israel, including David's older brothers lined up in battle.

But, the Philistines had a champion named Goliath who the whole army was afraid to fight. He was nine feet tall and it seemed like he could defeat anyone. Goliath would stand between the Philistine army and Saul's army and yell out threat and taunts. All of Saul's army was terrified of him.

One day, David came to check on his brothers and bring them food.
David heard Goliath yelling.
David couldn't believe that someone would talk like that about God's people.
David also couldn't believe that no one dared to fight him.

David approached the king and said he would go fight Goliath. King Saul laughed and offered David his armor. But, David walked out toward Goliath with nothing but his sling and five smooth stones.

As David approached Goliath, he said,
"You come against me with sword and spear,
but I come in the name of the LORD **ALMIGHTY**.
The Lord will deliver you into my hands.
Everyone will know that the battle is the Lord's."

David put a stone in the sling and it hit Goliath on the forehead, knocking him down. Then, David killed Goliath with Goliath's own sword. On that day, God fought for his people through a young man.

So, is it time yet?

You might think that David is the Promised Rescuer by the way he rescued God's people from the Philistines, but David himself said that it was God who fought for them.

One day, God Himself came to earth and fought for His people again, rescuing them from their forever enemy, the serpent.

1 Samuel 17

Years passed and kings continued to rule over God's people. Some, well a few, pointed the people back to God. But, most of the kings drew the people further and further away from God. God's land was divided. God's people were far from Him and many were worshipping false gods.

1 Kings 18

Then God raised up a prophet named Elijah. God sent Elijah to speak to King Ahab. Elijah told him that all the trouble in Israel was because the people were worshipping false gods.

Elijah asked King Ahab to meet him on Mt. Carmel with 450 prophets of Baal (the false god) to prove who the real God was.

Elijah built an altar to God and put a bull on top of it, but he didn't light the fire. The prophets of Baal did the same thing. Elijah said that the God who lit the bull on fire was the true God.

For hours the prophets of Baal danced around their altar and prayed and shouted "Baal, answer us!" But, Baal did nothing.

After that, Elijah poured 12 barrels of water over his bull, wood and altar. And then he prayed, "Lord, you are the God of Abraham, Isaac, and Israel. Show these people who you are, so they will know that you, Lord, are God."

Then fire from the Lord came down and burned the sacrifice, the wood, the stones, and the ground around the altar. When the people saw this, they fell down and said,

"THE LORD IS GOD!"

So, is it time yet?
On that day, God came down in fire to bring His people back to Himself. One day, years later, God came down as a baby. He lived with His people, died for His people, and has brought them back to God forever.

All the people in the world were getting further and further away from God.

God chose a man named Jonah and told him to go and warn the people of Nineveh. Jonah was told to tell them that they needed to

REPENT

or they would be destroyed.

Jonah didn't want to go to Nineveh. Jonah didn't like the people of Nineveh. Jonah didn't think God should give them a chance to repent and turn to God.

So, Jonah got on a boat going the other way. A HUGE storm came up and all the sailors were terrified. Jonah knew that this storm was God trying to get his attention.

Jonah told the sailors to throw him into the sea.

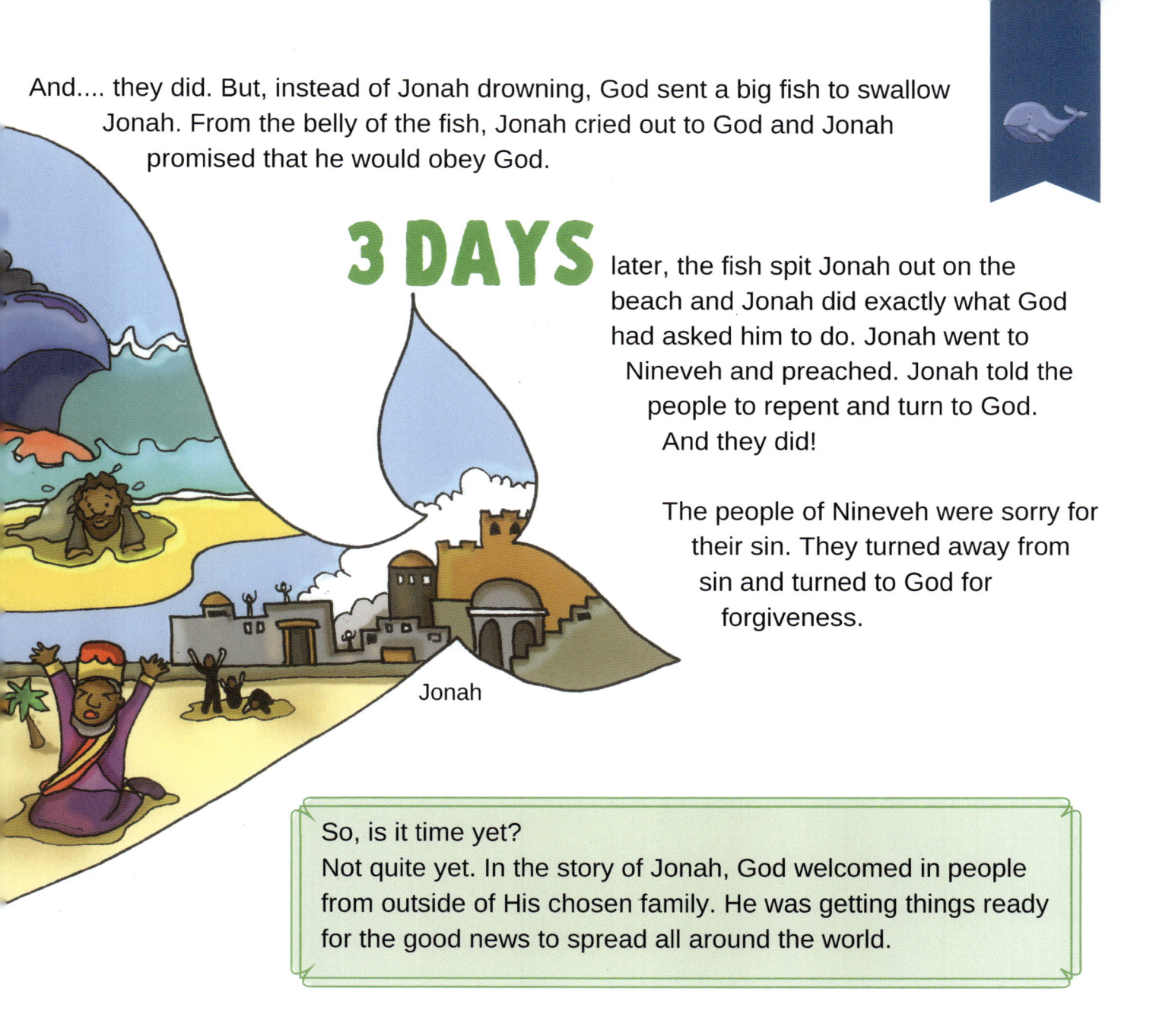

And.... they did. But, instead of Jonah drowning, God sent a big fish to swallow Jonah. From the belly of the fish, Jonah cried out to God and Jonah promised that he would obey God.

3 DAYS later, the fish spit Jonah out on the beach and Jonah did exactly what God had asked him to do. Jonah went to Nineveh and preached. Jonah told the people to repent and turn to God. And they did!

The people of Nineveh were sorry for their sin. They turned away from sin and turned to God for forgiveness.

Jonah

So, is it time yet?
Not quite yet. In the story of Jonah, God welcomed in people from outside of His chosen family. He was getting things ready for the good news to spread all around the world.

God's people were far from Him. They were more and more sinful. God had called them to be set apart and holy, like Him. But they were more and more like the world.

God had allowed His people to be taken captive by their enemies.
But God didn't forget them.
God kept sending prophets to call them back to Himself.
God kept sending prophets to remind them of the Rescuer He had promised.

One of these prophets was a man named Isaiah.
Isaiah came to God's people and told them all about the coming Rescuer. He told them to turn from their sin and turn back to Jesus.

He **PROPHESIED** about the coming Rescuer.

Isaiah said that the Rescuer would come from David's family.
Isaiah said that the Rescuer would be born to a virgin.
Isaiah said that the Rescuer would be the Wonderful Counselor, the Mighty God, the Everlasting Father and the Prince of Peace.

And most importantly, Isaiah said a **SON** would be given.

So, is it time yet?
Not yet. Once again, God reminded His people that He was sending the Rescuer. But the time wasn't right yet.

Isaiah 7, 9, 53

400

For generations and generations, God spoke with, lived with, and led His people.

Sometimes he spoke to them directly, like when He gave Moses the law.
Sometimes He spoke through judges like Samson and Samuel.
Sometimes He spoke through kings like David and Josiah.
Sometimes He spoke through prophets and messengers like Isaiah and Jonah.

But then, God stopped speaking. For 400 years God did not speak to His people.
There were no prophets.
There were no messengers.

God was **SILENT.**

God's people still had the promises.
    They remembered the promise of a Rescuer.
    They remembered the promise of a Son.
    They remembered the promise of a Forever King.

But they remembered in silence. All they could do was **WAIT.**

So, is it time yet?
No. God's people were waiting. God's people were trusting and hoping in silence. They were hoping that God would break the silence just like He did when He spoke the world into being. And when He did, He broke the silence with the announcement of a baby to be born.

400

And then one night, God sent a messenger to **MARY.**

Mary was a young girl, a virgin.
She was engaged to marry a man named
Joseph, but they weren't married yet.

An angel appeared to her and told her that God was with her!

She couldn't believe her ears.
No one had heard from God for years, and now God had a message for her.

And this was the angel's message:
"God has chosen you.
You will have a baby boy and you will name him Jesus.
He is the Son of God and He is the Promised One you've been waiting for.
Jesus is the Promised Rescuer. Jesus is the Forever King."

Mary didn't think this could be possible, but the angel assured her that it was true.
This was God's plan. This was the **FULFILLMENT**
of all of God's promises.

The rescue they had been waiting on was coming.
God Himself was coming to their rescue!

> So, is it time yet?
> Almost! The Promised One was on His way, but in a very unexpected way.

Luke 1

Finally, on a dark night, in the little town of Bethlehem, a baby was born. The Promised One was here.

He came into the world like every other baby, but was he like every other baby? This baby was fully God and fully man.

The **SON OF GOD** had come into the world.

When he was born, Mary and Joseph wrapped Him tightly in cloths and laid him in a manger.

And, just like after the birth of every other baby, His birth was announced and people celebrated. But, instead of Mary and Joseph announcing His birth, His Father, God Himself, announced the birth of His Son.

God sent angels to announce Jesus' birth to shepherds out in the field. The angels said, "The Savior has been born." **"HE'S HERE."**

What an amazing announcement!

Then, the shepherds ran to celebrate the birth of the Savior and found Jesus lying in a manger just like the angels had told them.

> So, is it time yet?
> **YES!** He's here. The Promised One has arrived. The wait is over!

Luke 2

After waiting for the Promised One for so long, He's finally here!
But, our story isn't complete. You see, the story doesn't end with a baby in a manger.

Jesus came for one very specific
REASON.
Jesus came to earth to die on the cross.
Jesus came to pay the price for our sin.
Jesus came to rescue God's people once and for all.

And that's what He did. After living the sinless life that we could never live,

Jesus died the death that we deserved to die. You see, back in the garden, God was clear when He said the punishment for sin is death. Jesus died our death.

But He didn't only **DIE**, Jesus also **ROSE AGAIN.**
Now, all those who follow Jesus can live forever with Him!

So, is it time yet? **YES!**

The Messiah, the Promised One, came. He was born as a baby. He lived a perfect life and then He died on the cross to pay the price for our sin.

Now it's your time. Just like the prophets of the Old Testament called God's people to repent, this story calls you to turn to God and trust in Him.

This story calls you to believe in Jesus as the Promised Rescuer!

Luke 23 & 24

Hi. I'm Bethany. I spent 20 years working full-time in children's ministry, but now I focus on full-time ministry at home with my husband and 1-year-old son. During my years in children's ministry, I discovered gaps in the available curriculum and often struggled to find a curriculum that worked in my church setting. It was this discovery that awakened a passion in me for writing children's ministry curriculum and other gospel-driven resources for children and families. During nap times, I am the lead curriculum developer for the Sunday School Store. I'd love to connect with you on Facebook at 'Treasure Trunk Books' or on IG at 'Treasure_Trunk_Kids.' On these pages, I share articles and resources for families as well as what I'm doing to point my little one to Christ. I am also the author of 'Sing and Play Big Bible Truths,' designed to help parents point toddlers to Christ.

My name is Jedidjah although many know me as Didi . I'm the person behind the illustrations in this book . I live in South Africa with my husband and 3 daughters and a lot of animals. Photography has been my creative outlet of choice for the past 10 years, but after an unfortunate incident which involved a man and a gun who really wanted my camera earlier this year, I picked up my pencil and pen and redirected some creative energy into this book. Besides photography and drawing , I'm involved in a program called the Rare Bear project which empowers women in the informal settlement near where I live to earn an income through crocheting projects -you can check it out at www.facebook.com/RareBearsSA/. Five years ago I also started a page called " I have a Name " which has become a platform to get the stories of ordinary people out there and creates opportunities for people to come around them and help in various ways. You can find it at www.facebook.com/ihaveanamethisismystory/.

Printed in Great Britain
by Amazon